Social Media Mar[

7 Easy Steps to Master Social Media Advertising,

Influencer Marketing & Platform Audience Growth

Santino Spencer

More by Santino Spencer

Discover all books from the Marketing Management Series by Santino Spencer at:

bit.ly/santino-spencer

Themed book bundles available at discounted prices:

bit.ly/santino-spencer

Copyright

Table of Contents

Introduction

Welcome to *Social Media Marketing;* whether you are trying to run a business or just up your social media marketing game, you have made a great choice. The seven steps shared within *Social Media Marketing* will provide great value to enhance your success. Every business, regardless of size, has to have some type of strategy for social media marketing. Simply going about social media marking without a plan can be very costly and honestly might even hurt your brand.

Social media has become the fastest moving industry in the world. Businesses can grow faster, find new customers quicker, grow their wealth and knowledge by reaching out to people from all over the world. This is something that was not possible several decades ago when the only form of marketing accessible to most businesses was print, radio, and television advertising. Your reach was restricted based on your budget, and you had no control over how many times your target audience would listen or see the content you are putting out there. Well, not anymore.

One of social media's most powerful features is the way it can connect people from all over the world in a matter of seconds. It doesn't matter where you are located, as long as you have a working internet connection and some device to view content on, you're connected. For businesses, this has been an *incredible* advantage. Imagine the business potential when you can now reach millions of customers worldwide?

Social media has changed the world of marketing forever. For example, your business can go live in a matter of seconds to people across the world. Your product launch, when it is done as live broadcast, it is instantly shown to customers from every country imaginable. You get to share the amazing things that happen in your company with your loyal customers and build relationships with them in a way that you never could before social media came along.

This platform has forced businesses to become more creative, innovative, and more attentive to what the customers want in order to keep the content fresh, relevant, and appealing to the target audience. Social media has also become a hotbed of research, and this is where *your business* begins to transform your marketing strategies. The seven-step approach in the next few chapters will be your guide to marketing your business on this social, digital space like a winner. Let's get started.

Chapter 1: Step 1 – Understand Why Your Business Needs It

Social media is the king of the marketing world. There is no one out there who *has not* heard of social media and what an incredible force it can be. Companies have gone from being unknown to a household name through the sheer power of social media marketing alone. Since it was created, social media has changed and revolutionized the internet. Despite the pros and cons, there is no denying that every single business out there is going to need social media marketing to remain competitive.

More importantly, you need social media if you want to stay in business. Customers these days *expect* you to have some kind of social media presence before they can even think about taking you seriously. Let's put it this way, if your competitor has a social media presence and you don't, they are going to go to your competitors, no matter how fabulous your product may be.

What Is It?

Customers don't want to be handed flyers or brochures with your sales pitch on it anymore. Customers today are only going to be interested in what you have to sell if you find a way to engage with them in an interesting and relevant way. That is where social media comes into play. Social media marketing is basically marketing that is done on social media platforms. You will be using platforms like Facebook, Instagram, or Twitter, for example, to announce new product launches, introduce new services, talk about your latest line, and a whole lot more. Yes, it is that simple.

To be honest, it is not that far different from the old marketing methods that businesses and companies have been employing even before social media was a thing. It is still marketing, except this time, all the tools and techniques of marketing have been modified to accommodate social media platforms. You're marketing your products on social media instead of print, television, and radio this time.

Social media marketing is an approach that businesses can utilize to interact with their customers and potential customers in the most natural way possible. This can easily be done on the bigger, more popular platforms like Facebook and Twitter, and it can also be done on smaller niche sites that are built around communities. Think of social media as a town hall, where every customer comes together to share stories, ideas, thoughts, opinions, and feedback about a product or service. To touch base with new prospective customers that may be coming through your pipeline and convert them into loyal, paying customers, you need social media platforms to help you achieve that goal.

As for your customers, social media platforms are not marketing machines but social networks. When you start embarking on developing your social media marketing strategy, you may be up against a few challenges. Plenty of companies to in hard and start hard selling to their consumers, which inundates their followers with discount offer codes and new product announcement, even before consumers could even warm up to the brand. When their accounts do not bring the traffic they want, these brands assume that these networks aren't a good fit for them or social media isn't the place to spend their efforts on.

Why Your Business Needs It

There are several reasons why your business needs social media marketing, and these are some of the reasons why you should be utilizing this form of communication as soon as possible:

- ***Your Marketing Costs Go Down*** - This is probably one of the things businesses love most about social media platforms is the ability to reduce their marketing cost. Yes, it is going to reduce your marketing costs by *a lot.* Compared to traditional marketing methods like print advertising, television, billboards, magazines, or radio channels, marketing on social media is remarkably more affordable.

Don't forget that social media channels itself are *free,* and it does not cost anything to create a free social media account for your business to get the ball rolling.

- ***It Is the Best Way to Showcase Your Brand*** - Social media marketing is by far the best way to showcase your brand these days. In fact, it has become the number one way for a business to increase its brand recognition without having to spend a ton of money on traditional advertising methods. Social media marketing gives your business the opportunity to boost your reputation through your website, search engine optimization, email marketing, and more.

    It is an opportunity to drive sales and build relationships with your customers by interacting with them on a one-to-one level, something that was not possible before with traditional forms of marketing. What is even better is that you get to communicate with your customers through your social media pages for *free.* It costs you nothing to respond to their comments, chat messages, and queries. Each time you do that, you're building a connection with your customers, and in the business world, this form of communication and interaction is priceless.

- ***You're Developing a Loyal Following and Community*** - By creating these relationships with your customers, you are indirectly building a loyal community among them as you do this. People have always enjoyed being a part of something. People enjoy being part of a group, a crowd, a club, something that makes them feel a sense of belonging and acceptance. Today, businesses have the opportunity to create such a community among the people through social media marketing. Your customers will enjoy being associated with a brand that is actively building a lively community online, especially if they get to interact with other like-minded customers for some honest feedback and opinions about your products and services.

Customers want value for money these days, and reviews online alone are not going to cut it. They want recommendations and suggestions straight from the horse's mouth, and in this case, the proverbial horse would be the other customers. By building a community like this, you are helping your customers establish an emotional connection with your brand, and if you trigger the right emotions, you make them customers for life. This is the kind of relationship that is essential for your long-term success.

- **_Better Customer Service_** - A successful business is no longer about just the purchase and sale of products anymore. Customers expect more than merely purchasing your products and letting that be the end of the story. Oh no, these days, customers want to share their feedback and thoughts about your products, and social media is the best channel for them to do this. Not only does social media allow your customers to communicate directly with your company, but they can also communicate with each other. Word of mouth is one of the best forms of free marketing you can get your hands on.

There is nothing like a good word or recommendation from a source to have other customers flocking to your business, eager to get their hands on your products too. Plus, being able to communicate directly with your business helps to enhance your brand's trustworthiness while simultaneously improving your customer service. With the old way of marketing, a business was nothing more than a cold, distant entity to the customer. Today, businesses and customers can interact instantaneously with each other as old friends would.

- *It Increases Your Digital Exposure* - By actively interacting on your social media channels, you are significantly increasing your online presence. A customer will remember and prefer a business that is actively responding to their messages or comments within a reasonable timeframe. One of the reasons why social media is an incredible platform for maximizing your brand's exposure is because of its worldwide presence. It is accessible to everyone in the world with an internet connection and at least a smartphone.

Social media accounts are free to set up, and this means that every single one of your customers is ninety-nine percent very likely to own at least one type of social media account. In fact, a lot of shopping these days happens on social media accounts, not just websites alone anymore. The massive number of daily users and its incredible content-sharing capabilities means news about your business will spread in a matter of seconds. Five minutes from now, your brand name could be introduced to someone halfway across the world from you, all through the incredible power of social media.

- *It Helps to Boost Your Traffic and Search Engine Rating* - Social media platforms are major lead generators. They bring a consistent stream of high-volume traffic to your website and maximize your search engine optimization (SEO). Search engines can significantly reflect your social media content with the right keywords. This is potential that no business can afford to miss out on.

- *It Expands Your Sales and Reaches New Groups of Audiences Quickly* - Nothing else can generate new sales and reach new customers as quickly as social media can, once again, thanks to its incredible worldwide reach. By monitoring and listening to the conversations that are happening on your social media pages *from your customers,* this is an opportunity to address their needs *specifically.* Businesses never had this opportunity before social media came along. Back then, you could only guess the specifics of what your customer wanted based on surveys or questionnaires. By addressing what they need, it expands your sales and increases your customer base.

Traditional forms of marketing, while still being used today, are slowly on their way out. It is the age of the internet where everything is online, everything is immediate, and almost everyone is accessible with just a few clicks of the mouse. Social media platforms are the easiest and most convenient way for people to keep in touch even if they may be halfway across the globe. Businesses realize that today's consumer is shifting away from those old advertising forms. Today, the attention is on social media platforms, and this is where you need to be. You need to go where your customers are.

Chapter 2: Step 2 - Market Research Done Right

Did you know that social media marketing could be used for in-depth information into your market research process? For any business, it is important that your product or service is all about the consumer. Everything that you do should be all about your customers. This is where market research plays a vital role in keeping up with what your customers want and expect from your business. Since they are paying money for your products and services, they will be expecting you to provide what they are looking for.

What Is Social Media Market Research?

This is the type of research that acknowledges your branding and the way that your business is reaching your target audience. In other words, it tells you whether your marketing campaigns are effectively progressing the way that you hoped it would. It gives you insight into the marketing methods you have been using on each of your social media platforms in the past, present, and future. The research conducted will point out whether your efforts have been effective in achieving your business goals.

The Benefits of Market Research

For the answers to your *who, what, where, when, why*, and *how* questions, you need market research. Market research is a valuable tool that has long been used by businesses to better understand the needs and demands of their target audience base. Thanks to social media, however, not only do businesses get to research what their customers are up to, they also get to research what their competitors are doing too. The kiss of death for any business is to assume that they know that the customers' needs are, or to assume that they should just go ahead and build a business first, and the marketing will take care of bringing the customers in. That is just a warrant for failure.

In the business world, every single decision that is being made in the interest of the business needs to have a foundation on concrete and undeniable research proof behind it, even for campaigns that are being run on social media. Besides giving you intel into the minds of your customers, market research is beneficial for the following reasons:

- It keeps you focused on your business plan and ensures that you are always looking ahead at what the next step should be.

- It reminds you to listen to your target audience whenever you're thinking about coming up with a new product or service line. Give the people what they want, and they will keep coming back to you for more.

- It tells you what problems you need to solve for your customers and helps you create the right product to get the job done.

- Market research helps you identify what your business opportunities are. When you know what the customer wants, you can start strategizing about what needs to be done to meet those needs and demands. This puts you in a unique position to take advantage of opportunities your competition may not have had a chance to yet.

- Market research ensures that you stay relevant, and in doing so, you keep your business relevant. Staying relevant and keeping your customers loyal is about being able to meet and fulfill the needs that they have. If they don't get it from your business, they will get it from your competitors, and there is no amount of marketing you can do that will keep your customers with you if you are not meeting their needs.

- It cuts down on the risks and losses you experience per campaign. Research supplies your business with the necessary and vital information you need to decide on what the right approach or the next step should be. This keeps the risks to a minimum because you will not be stumbling blindly forward hoping that their plan is going to work. With your research in hand, you will know for a fact what the right move should be because they have the research on hand to back it up.

- Market research helps to point out what your current and potential business issues are. As a business, you need to pay close attention to the feedback that is being received by your market research audience because oftentimes, they will be able to shed light on an area that may not even be seen as a problem for the company but raises issues with its target market.

- Market research makes your customers feel happy because it tells them that your business is listening to their concerns. When customers feel that they are being heard and that a business is taking the time to find out what they want, there is a higher chance that they will remain loyal to the businesses.

Primary and Secondary Market Research

Market research is divided into two categories, primary and secondary. Primary market research is the most important type of research for your business. It is research that is done in real-time, and it is research that you are doing yourself. Primary research is where you start from scratch with information that does not exist yet. Not until you create it. You are conducting this research to find the information and data that you need. Traditionally, primary market research was a costly affair. It was conducted through focus groups, interviews, and surveys. In this aspect, social media has been a complete game-changer. With social media, the valuable primary market research information you need can be collected *for free.* You can conduct polls on social media for free, conduct interviews with special guests on your live streams and make a note of the questions your customers ask, and much more.

Your secondary research is information that already exists, like your customers' interests based on their profiles, the types of questions they've already asked you. All you have to do is analyze the existing research to see how you can use it to your advantage. Examples of where you would go for secondary research include case studies conducted by your competitors if the information is available online, tuning in to your competitor's live streams, or analyzing the results from previous campaigns and surveys you have conducted in the past.

Both primary and secondary research have their benefits, but primary research has a more personalized factor to it. Plus, primary research gives you access to the latest information that is relevant to your customers. Today, you can run polls on your Facebook and Instagram stories. It only takes mere seconds for your customers to quickly tap on the answers they prefer, and there you go. You have instant answers to your questions. The authenticity of the information you gather from this approach is extraordinary. For example, by showcasing different products across your Instagram or Facebook

Stories feature throughout the week, you might be surprised to learn which are your most popular and least popular products. With access to information like this, you can instantly revise your key selling points and campaign focus as you go.

Social Media Channels That Are Good for Research

The different social media channels can provide insight and contribute to your research in various ways:

- *Facebook Groups* - Join a Facebook group that your target audience is part of and start participating in the discussions. If you prefer to be a passive observer that just watches and reads what people are talking about in these groups, you can do that too. Facebook Groups also give you the option of using question polls as part of your research. You can type out a question (a primary market research method) and get the answers that you are looking for to help you develop your next content or product.

- *Twitter* - Twitter allows you the option of creating lists. You can put your target audience on these lists, either on one list or a couple of different lists, depending on what your research objective is. Having these lists makes it easier for you to scroll through to find out what your customer interests are, what content they are tweeting about, the hashtags they use, and more. You also have the option of creating a competitor's list, where you put your competitors on a specific list to go through to research the type of content they are putting out, the hashtags they use, and the content they are tweeting about too.

- *YouTube* - On YouTube, you can source for content that is similar to yours and go through the comments section to see the types of questions that are being asked. You can find out a surprising amount of information about your target audience this way, like the types of problems they have and the answers they are looking for. By going through these comments, it can help you develop content that *they* are interested in, enticing them to your page instead of your competitor's.

- *Live Streams* - These Live Streams are available on most social media platforms. It notifies your followers when your business is broadcasting live. For example, once you start your live stream, your customers that follow your account are going to get a notification on their phone saying you've gone live, and they'll quickly tune in to your content. This is a fantastic approach to conducting some immediate market research by conducting a question and answer session.

- *Surveys* - This one is a traditional marketing tactic that has existed even before the days of the internet. Surveys are a primary market research method that is still being used today because it still has a purpose. Websites like Survey Monkey make it easy to quickly create a free survey that you can quickly send to your customers. You can post your survey on your Facebook page, website, Instagram, and other social media platforms that you prefer.

Chapter 3: Step 3 - How to Market on Facebook

You could be just starting out with your Facebook marketing tactics, or you could be a seasoned marketer. Either way, every business is always on the lookout for ways to improve their marketing strategies so they can market on Facebook like a winner. Whether your goal is to boost your following or engagement rate, no matter what your goals are, you need to have the right strategies in order to make it work. Facebook is a crowded space with millions of contents being shared daily by individual users and businesses alike. The only way to be a winner in this platform is to stand out with the right marketing tactics.

Your Content Is Where the Magic Happens

Facebook is your platform, but your content is where the magic happens. If you want your content to stand out, it has to be incredible. There is a lot of content that gets posted on Facebook daily, and this means it is going to take something remarkable to make an impression on your target audience. Your content is not the only one they will be exposed to on a daily basis, and it is important that you make a strong enough first impression with every piece of content you post if you want your business to stay at the forefront of their minds.

As businesses, brands, and marketers, quality content should be your focal point with everything that you post. Before you hit the publish button, the question you need to ask yourself is, *"is my content worth noticing?"*. A good tip to keep in mind when you are trying to create and curate your quality content is to focus on a niche. Instead of trying to target the billions of users on Facebook, even though it is tempting to try and bring in as many customers as possible, you will be much better off targeting a subset of users instead. This makes it much easier to produce useful content that is equally entertaining to this niche group. When you know who you are targeting and what they want to see from you, it makes it easier to come up with quality content that matters.

Another way to create quality content is to focus on what your goals are. For example, if your goal was to drive traffic to your website, then you would focus on content that is specifically designed to encourage your target audience to flock to your website. Having goals in mind gives you a purpose, and with that purpose, you can begin creating the type of content you need to meet those goals. For effective marketing, ninety percent of your time should be spent on creating content, while the other ten percent of that time is focused on posting the content. Avoid the mistake of getting too caught up with trying to post as much as possible in the hopes of staying relevant on your audience's page. They would much rather see you post once a day but posting something that is useful to them, instead of posting frivolous content five times a day. It is not the quantity; it is the quality that matters.

Focus on Creating Video Content

The majority of your audience these days is going to be more interested in video content over everything else. Mark Zuckerberg himself once said that videos are the future of social media. Facebook's algorithm even focuses on placing video content at the top of the newsfeed. If you were to analyze your statistics over the course of a few months, you would probably notice that your video content is going to see the most successful compared to any other type of content you produce. You don't need a lot of resources or a big team to create quality video content. In fact, it is much easier than you think, and quality content begins by keeping these few tips in mind when you're making your videos:

- Avoid being too "sales-y" with your videos. Videos should be used as a brand awareness tool, not a sales pitch.

- Keep your videos to a maximum of two minutes. The top-performing videos on this platform are usually between sixty and ninety seconds long.

- Keep the captions in your videos between fifty to a hundred characters. Your audience does not have time to read long and lengthy captions. Ideally, you want your captions to capture the gist of the overall message.

Another important factor to keep in mind is that more than ninety percent of your audience is most likely going to be viewing your content on their mobile phones. This means that your target audience would be scrolling through their feed quickly, and therefore, they don't have time for long and lengthy content. Users have very short attention spans, and they will easily be distracted by other things going on around them. To win them over, you need to keep your videos short, to the point, and put your *best content* at the *front of your video.* You only have seconds to intrigue your audience enough to make them watch your video all the way through, and you need to make those first few seconds count.

Why You Should Be Sharing Curated Content

Creating new content is time-consuming, and despite your best efforts, there may be times when you are so busy running the business that you simply don't have time to create new content. To supplement this, what you could do is share curated content. Share content from another top, reputable source that is from within your industry. You don't have to worry about replacing the content strategy of your own business when you do this. Sharing curated content is merely a supplement to help you maintain a consistent voice and posting on social media.

There is a benefit to sharing curated content from other sources too. If all you do is post content about your business all the time, people are going to start tuning you out after a while because it is all the same thing. There is nothing that keeps it fresh, interesting, and exciting on your page. By sharing curated content from others, you are strengthening your position as an industry leader, showing your audience your vast knowledge on the subject. Another benefit of doing this is that you get to build relationships with the people whose content you are sharing.

Repurpose Your Top Performing Content

Do you have content that has performed well in the past? Why not share it again? Not all your users are going to see every piece of content that you post. There is no harm in re-sharing old content. The one rule of thumb to keep in mind when you do this is to wait at least a month before you re-share any piece of content. Allow some time to pass before you put this post up again. Ideally, you would want a never-ending supply of fresh, new, and great content you can post to your Facebook page. However, since this is not always the case, your next best option would be to re-share what already proved to be popular in the past.

Focus on Your "Pages to Watch"

This is one of the most powerful tools you can use to create great social media content. You will get access to your "Pages to Watch" feature once you have seventy-five likes or more on your page. With this feature, you get to watch up to a hundred pages. It could be your competitors, inspirational pages that you love, and any sort of page you would like. Once you have a list of pages that you can find inspiration from daily, you can use this for ideas to guide your own Facebook strategy. The top three ways to use this "Pages to Watch" feature include the following:

- You could use this as a guide to set goals and benchmarks for your own brand. For example, you could use it to set audience engagement or growth goals.

- You could use this feature to curate content. Facebook even ranks the most popular type of content first, literally making your job easier by telling you what content has proven to be the most popular on other similar pages.

Listen to Your People

A lot of businesses will say that they struggle to come up with content. Why do they struggle? Because they are not listening to their audience. One of the most important foundations of any marketing strategy, whether it is social media or conventional marketing techniques, is listening to your target market. If you listen to your people, they will *tell you what they want to see and hear from you.* You don't have to spend hours brainstorming new and fresh ideas, all you have to do is learn to listen. Once you have gathered these details, you can create content that is tailored to their interests and needs and spark conversations that lead to sales.

Chapter 4: Step 4 - How to Market on Instagram

If you want your Instagram following to grow, it is important to have a strategy that works. This rule of thumb can be applied to all your social media platforms, truth be told. Instagram is a platform that is focused heavily on visual content. It is less about the captions and more about the captivating images. Just like Facebook, this platform is also one of the stronger social media tools for marketing and brand building, although it uses a different approach. Instagram's core strengths lie in its vivid imagery gallery, and for businesses like retailers, clothing companies, jewelry companies, travel companies, and any business that relies heavily on presenting itself through images, this is an excellent social media platform to do so. Instagram should be treated as a marketing tool and part of your entire overall marketing strategy. It may be a powerful social media platform, but it is not a standalone method for building your business.

Instagram has the potential to generate hundreds of new customers each month, but only if you're going about it the right way.

You Need to Have a Plan

You need to have a plan because it is going to guide your efforts and point you in the right direction. Your outcome is going to be a lot more fruitful if you have a good sense of where you should be going.

When you are developing your marketing strategy, spend some time thinking about what your primary goal with your Instagram account is. Avoid simply snapping and recording anything just for the sake of appearing active on your social media account. In order to post successfully captivating images and videos, the content needs to tell a story. All images and videos that get posted on Instagram will be a reflection of your business, and therefore, you want each content you put out there to link back to your overall business goals.

Here's a hint you might not have thought about. Your goal *should not be* trying to grow your following. That's right, you need to think bigger than that. Your goals should be along the lines of getting more traffic to your website, building your email list, boosting the sales of your products or service, and not about how many likes you can get on a picture you posted this morning or how many followers you've gained. Of course, it is always good news to see your numbers growing in terms of followers. It means your business is getting noticed, but there is a lot more potential to be tapped into with Instagram. Think bigger with your goals and use Instagram to help you reach those goals.

Create Shareable Content

What most businesses would do is create content that is focused entirely on their business. Of course, that is what you should be doing, isn't it? Are you only creating content that is all about you? Well, not necessarily. What you should do instead is create content that other people can share.

Identify Who Your Target Market Is

Not sure who your target market is? Then you have work to do. Like all social media platforms, you need to know who your target market is because it is an important element of your business. Your customers are the lifeline of your business, and if you target the wrong groups, you're wasting all the time, energy, and resources you committed to marketing on Instagram. Since Instagram can be a rather time-consuming platform, you want to make sure that everything you do on this platform has a purpose.

Since Instagram is limited to visual postings, you need to think about how to take your connection with your followers a step further by reaching out even more. One example of how you do this is to provide a link in your description section that directs back to your company's website or landing page. A lot of websites these days have a call to action feature the minute a user lands on their site by either asking them to simply subscribe to a newsletter.

This is why it is important to identify your target market. When a user subscribes, companies get access to the user's email, and this will then allow them to send updates and reach out to the users directly into their inbox. When posting images and videos on your social media platform, prompt the audience with a call to action by redirecting them back to the link on your bio. Your target market will be the group of people who will benefit the most from your offerings. This is going to be different for every business, depending on what your brand and your business represent. Identify as much information as you can about your target market, and this will allow you to create content that is specifically relevant to what they want to see from you.

Your Account Needs to Be Visible

Avoid the mistake of making your account private. You would be surprised at how often this little detail gets overlooked. Privatizing your personal account is fine, but your business account should remain as accessible as possible. Your target customers and audience base need to be able to locate you on Instagram, and it won't help if your account is private, and they have no access to the content your business offers unless they follow your account. Your target customers don't want to feel like they are being forced into joining or following your business, they want to be able to choose it. Make your content visible and easy to find on the social media platform, and make it likable enough that the audience wants to keep tabs with what you're doing by being a follower.

Use Your Hashtags Sparingly

Hashtags are the most popular on Instagram, although Twitter and Facebook do incorporate the use of hashtags on their platforms as well, it was never still quite as popular as it is on Instagram. In fact, one of the primary ways of discovering a new person, product, group, or business on Instagram is through hashtags. Hashtags are one of Instagram's main marketing strengths because not only does it make it easy for users to discover a business, businesses also find it easier to track potential consumers. Avoid being tempted to bombard your post with every single hashtag that pops into your mind. Focus on the ones that link back to your business.

Customers and audiences who are on the lookout for something specific will have a better chance of locating your content when the right hashtags have been put into place. The key tip here is to ensure everything posted, from content to texts and hashtags are in unison and complement one another. Before posting any content, it's recommended that you look at the trending hashtags of the day and narrow down the ones that are related to your business and content. If it's relevant then go ahead and use it, but if it's not, then ditch it.

Create Content That Is Strategic

Once you deeply understand who your target audience is, creating content that matters becomes a whole lot easier. Every photo, video, and the caption that you take should speak directly to your customer.

Be clear about what your business is offering. Your content should offer a solution and provide value to your customers and your followers. If your target customers and the audience are not sure of what your business is selling, you lose the potential to gain new customers because they will lose interest.

People like to know what they're dealing with, and businesses who don't have a strong, clear presence and message are going to be on the losing end. When you aim to create content specifically for a demographic, you are going to naturally attract them to your Instagram feed. They will decide that they *want* to follow you because they can relate to everything that you post. When your content makes them feel like you are speaking directly to them, it can convert them into loyal, paying customers. If you create random content, you might end up attracting a mix of people and get a higher number of followers, but they might not take the action that you want.

Engage with Your Target Audience Regularly

To consistently attract the right kind of audience who will take the action you want, you need to engage with your target market regularly.

Create Vertical Video Content

Video marketing is a must for anyone running a business. Many successful businesses acknowledge that videos are crucial and a necessary tool as part of their overall marketing strategy. To make the best impact possible on your viewers, you need to fully utilize the video marketing capabilities on Instagram. Thanks to videos being primarily shot on smartphones these days by users themselves, the vertical video trend has increased in popularity so much that they outperform the horizontal videos in every way.

It's a mobile world out there. Users are on their mobiles more than their desktops these days. At the end of each video, don't forget to include a call to action that will ask and remind your audience to take a specific action. A call to action encourages your audience to take the next step toward your primary goal and move along in your marketing funnel.

Chapter 5: Step 5 - How to Market on YouTube

What videos should you make for your business's YouTube channel? How will your target audience find you? Where do you even begin making content that is going to get your business noticed and skyrocket your marketing goals? It all comes down to three key things:

- Your strategy
- How to set up your channel
- How to secure your first few subscribers

Your YouTube Marketing Strategy

YouTube is one of the best platforms for business to engage with current and prospective customers because not only is YouTube a cost-effective marketing platform, but it has a much bigger reach than any other video dissemination platform out there. With more than a billion users to date and counting, this is one marketing opportunity you cannot afford to pass up.

YouTube is such an easy marketing tool for businesses to make use of because of how easy it is to share videos online. YouTube videos are also easily shareable on other social media platforms, which makes it easy for businesses to promote the content many times over on their other social media accounts like Facebook and Twitter, doubling or tripling a YouTube video's reach just like that.

Now, the number one mistake that a lot of companies make with YouTube is not creating content *and thumbnails* that are interesting enough. Yes, your thumbnails have to be equally attractive because that is the first thing your customers will look at. Would you click on a thumbnail that didn't intrigue you? Probably not, and your customers will think the same. Many businesses get so caught up in creating interesting content of value that they forget they need to make their thumbnails attractive on their profile too.

The first step in creating a marketing strategy on YouTube is just like any other social platform, and it begins with defining your goals. With YouTube, you want to write down specific targets that you want to achieve, such as clicks and traffic, engagement as well as reach and subscriber numbers. If you want your audience to watch your videos, then you need to make videos that they *want to watch.* Otherwise, they are not going to watch, it is as simple as that.

The questions to ask when you're thinking about crafting your YouTube strategy for your video content are:

- What value can I add to my videos that the customer would appreciate?
- What is my target audience interested in?

- What videos would my target audience be willing to watch willingly without them feeling like they are being forced into it?

Value is added to your videos by *teaching* your audience something new, something useful, and something that will benefit them. You also add value by entertaining them through your videos and triggering emotions. How-to videos are among the high-performing videos on YouTube because they provide plenty of value to users. Since YouTube is the second most used search engine, people go to YouTube because they want to see something done or learn how to make something or cook something or build something.

How-To videos are great for plenty of business, no matter what industry you are in. If you are using this format, you need to look at what aspect of your business can be turned into a "How-To." For instance, you sell car engine oil. You can do a tutorial on how to use this oil, how to change your car engine oil, and the benefits of good oil. Look upon the internet for blog posts for materials you can use to create your video. Make this video edutainment.

Setting Up Your Channel

There are two types of channels you can set up. The first type of channel is where you have your profile as your main channel. The second channel is your brand channel. You need to set up a brand channel to gain access to the features you need to share with your employees and other people in the company who are also working on maintaining your channel. Every channel needs to have the following design elements:

- Your profile picture
- Your channel image
- Custom thumbnails (remember, your thumbnails need to be just as interesting and engaging as your videos)

An important note to keep in mind is that you need the elements on your channel to be consistent. Your brand needs to be represented in all your content. There are several ways you can optimize your channel too, and some of these elements are within your control, and some are not. Keywords that you use and how you use them are completely in your control, however, elements like how many people subscribe immediately after viewing your videos are not exactly things that you can control or have power on.

Going back to the importance of thumbnails, the right kind of thumbnail will attract a reader to click on it, making your video trend as well as make your channel recognizable. Just like the title, your thumbnail should be relevant to the content as well as correspond with your video title. Attractive thumbnails result in higher clicks. You should also include short descriptions in your thumbnail so viewers can understand what your video is all about. You want to immediately catch the interest of your viewers by telling them a quick story just by your thumbnails and your title. Not only should these elements tell viewers what your video is all about, but it should also make them curious enough to want to watch your videos. Make a template or style guide for your thumbnails to maintain consistency here too.

Getting Your First Few Subscribers

Getting your first few subscribers is usually one of the biggest challenges that a company would face on YouTube. In such a vast space with millions of videos all vying for your attention, how do you get your content to stand out enough that people *want* to subscribe to your channel? This is even more important if you're already a big and established brand since it can look rather unprofessional if you only have a few subscribers. Well, the first step is easy, and that is to leverage your existing social media accounts. Use your Facebook, Twitter, Instagram, newsletters, and blogs to get the ball rolling. Try to send the existing audience there over to your channel.

Another thing that you could do is to work together with other channels and other YouTubers. Video collaboration is popular among YouTubers, and it is a great way to gain a new audience base as well as increase your subscriber base. It is a win-win situation for both YouTubers as well as the target audience since the audience will get to see their favorite YouTubers together working on something or creating something. Working with influencers is not an uncommon strategy. In fact, many brands are starting to leverage the potential that working with influencers can bring to their business. Collaboration has so many obvious advantages, so long as you do it with the right people and brands.

Social media influencers are powerful. They can drive traffic to your Facebook page overnight by simply putting in a few good words and a well-crafted video upload. Especially if they're demonstrating how your product is being used. According to Forbes, what they revealed was that MuseFind, an influencer marketing platform, found that audiences were ninety-two percent more likely to trust the word of a social media influencer compared with an ad. Sometimes, these brands or people don't necessarily have to be in your industry, and you could try looking for complimenting brands and influencers to work with as this will grow your audience exponentially. The potential for content creation here is enormous.

Collaboration is one of the very best ways to add some entertainment value to your content. Apart from connecting with your audience, you can also use social media to connect with experts, influencers, and industry leaders, thus enhancing your status as an authoritative expert and credible source of information for your industry. The huge rise of social media platforms has also given birth to a new trend of social media influencers. These influencers use their popularity to market products and services to generate income.

An influencer is an individual who has huge popularity or followers that listen or emulate them. They collaborate with marketers to promote products, services, and even events to their followers. This has pushed many ad agencies to increase their budget on social media influencer marketing to catch this trend. A social media influencer is described as someone who has a lot of followers online. They are generally an expert or an authority on a particular subject, although celebrities fall under the influencer category too because of the immense pull they have. What an influencer buys, wears, or says can influence the decision of their followers. Over time, you are more than just a brand, you are part of a community. This change of perception also leads towards higher ROI, which means you'll also get plenty of exposure. With higher ROI, you get more exposure, and with more exposure, comes leads and new leads turn into followers. These followers turn into potential customers.

Chapter 6: Step 6 - Focusing on the Right Niche Market

Everyday there are thousands of people are searching for various products and services to buy. They might need these products and services to help fulfil a need or want that they have. Your job as a business is to find the right people who are looking for the kind of products and services that you offer. Those specific people are your niche market group.

What Is a Niche Market?

A niche market is a group of people who are looking for a specific product. For example, if your business was selling health supplements, your niche market would be that specific group of people who were looking for the kind of health supplements you provide. Your niche market would depend on the kind of products and services that you sell. Another example would be if you were in the business of selling baby products. Baby products can be divided into a few categories, like baby shoes, clothing, food, bath products, and more. Baby shoes would be one of the niche market consumers you would target.

If you want to grow your business and achieve all your goal milestones, then you need to be focused on marketing to your niche audience. The logic behind this is simple, if your audience is far too broad and general, a lot of your efforts could be wasted on targeting those who are not even remotely interested in your content. The narrower and more niche your target audience is, the better your return on investment will be. This will help you write better content, more compelling posts, and more engaging information. These benefits, however, extend beyond marketing. You create brand loyalty and credibility, it helps you identify customer pain points, create a loyal following, refine product strategies, and improve sales conversions. To be effective with your marketing strategy, you need to aim for where it matters the most. This strategy will end up saving you a lot of time, money, and effort in the long run.

How Do You Find Your Niche Market?

It would depend once again on the kind of products or services you sell. The first thing you need to do is to find a focus. Niche marketing is all about focus. It is a focus on selling and advertising your strategies towards a targeted portion of the market. You do not market to everyone who could benefit from your product or service. Instead, you niche market your products to specific people, focusing exclusively on a group of people or a demographic section of likely customers that would most definitely enjoy or benefit from your products. If you are a writer, you could narrow your focus by limiting your writing to children's books. From there, you can narrow your focus even further by focusing only on books for little girls. You could get even more specific by defining the age range you want to target. The more specific you get with your targeting, the more niche your target market becomes.

You could target your audience based on geographic area, lifestyle, occasion, profession, style, culture, activity or habits, behavior, demographic, need, and more. The biggest concern that businesses have when it comes to niche marketing is the fear of losing out on thousands of potential customers. By narrowing your focus like that, you might be concerned that other people are missing out on your products, and therefore, you are missing out on a potential sale. This is a catch twenty-two because the answer is both yes and no. Not every business can be as booming as Amazon is, selling products that cater to practically everyone on the planet. Even if you do want to be like Amazon, Amazon didn't start out that way in the beginning. They had a specific niche they were focusing on too, and they sold books. Over time, they eventually progressed to the Amazon that we know and love today, where they are selling products in almost every category.

When you define a niche for yourself, you enter into a market with potentially less competition. Niche marketing's biggest benefit would be that it allows brands to stand out from the pack and appear unique. This will make sure it resonates better with its already unique and distinct customer section. A brand can employ niche marketing initiatives to stand out and be more valuable rather than blend in, to reach a higher growth potential and ultimately build a better, stronger, and long-lasting relationship with its target market. When you have a shoestring budget, or you're just getting started in the business world, minimal competition is good news, and that is why you should start out by focusing on a niche.

How do you determine what is the best niche market for your business? Through a lot of research, for one thing. There is going to be a lot of research that is going to go into this stage of your business, but it has to be done. You need to research, compare, and evaluate the current market trends and what you have to work with. When researching prices of items for example, look at several platforms instead of focusing on just one. For example, research current trends on Amazon and eBay, but don't make those the only platforms that you are looking at. Broaden your search to include different types of niches. Look at the higher-priced bracket items, and compare that to the lower bracket items. Compare and evaluate the market trends that you are observing on this platform. What is selling well and what isn't. What trends seem to be doing well and why? The more areas of your business that your research covers, the better.

Finding the right niche is also much easier when you aim to answer the following questions. More importantly, this framework is going to help you find a *profitable niche.* These questions are something that every business can use as a framework to find their target audience. The questions to ask as you seek to pinpoint your niche market include:

- *You Need to Figure Out Who You Would Like to Speak To (Who)* - Who are you talking to? This question needs to be answered before you come up with any kind of marketing campaign or catch-y tagline. If you don't know who you are talking to specifically, how would you know what you need to say?

- *What Problem Are You Trying to Solve? (What)* - What pain point does your business aim to solve with the products and services that you sell? Who are the customers out there with the same kind of problem? The customers who are looking for a product like yours to help them solve this pain point? That will tell you who your niche market is and the group that you should be targeting. There is a good chance that your product or service could solve more than one problem. If that is the case, what you should do as you try to pinpoint your niche in the early stages is to narrow it to one core problem that you want to focus on.

- *Be Specific About Your Benefits (Why)* - When crafting out your marketing message for your niche audience, you need to highlight the benefits of your products. Why should your customer be buying from you? How is your product going to change their life for the better? If the benefit of your product is something that is only found within your product, you should highlight this point when marketing to your niche.

- ***Brainstorm Who Will Be the Most Interested in Your Products*** - Talk to like-minded business friends who could give you some other insight, or perhaps even more ideas, maybe even have a brainstorming session or two with them. Talk to friends and family who are supportive because they too may be able to come up with some pretty good ideas that you could work with. Brainstorming sessions should be done as often as you feel it is necessary. Set a time for it, block out your calendar for a couple of hours to commit to this brainstorming focus entirely on that. Write down everything you know about possible session, and niche options, list them down in order of competition, loyalty, pricing, returns, and more. Compare and contrast which niche is going to give you the best returns, and you may have your answer in front of you on those pieces of paper where you just poured out all your ideas.

- ***Have You Tried Looking on Amazon?*** - As one of the biggest retailers in the world, Amazon sells just about everything on its platform. Thanks to the presence and reputation it has built for itself over the years, this is now one of the best platforms that you could use at your disposal to find a profitable niche market for your own business. Searching for a potential niche on Amazon is easy. All you would need to do is simply click the "All" tab that is located on the left side of the main search bar, and from there, you will easily find a list of categories which you can select from. Simply find a niche category that grabs your interest, click the "Go" button, and wait for the new page to pop up. On the left side of that page, you will then see the option to select a "sub-niche" category, and by clicking that link, you will be able to view even more specific sub-niches. It's a great platform to source for potential options, and the best part is you will be able to view which products are doing and selling well. Searching for best-selling products is easy. All you would need to do is click on the "Best Sellers" tab from the navigation bar, and there you go.

Chapter 7: Step 7 - Build an Unforgettable Presence

If we strike small talk with a random person, and we find the conversation stimulating and interesting, it will often lead to a full-blown conversation. This is a face-to-face scenario, and more often than not, face-to-face conversations get a little bit more time to convince the other person to listen to you but online communication? Communication on social media? Well, that's another story entirely.

You see, getting someone's attention on social media, or specifically getting your target user's attention on social media is much harder than approaching them and talking to them. Average users only need 8 seconds before they decide the content, they are viewing is not for them. This ultimately means that your conversations on social media not only has to be engaging, it also has to be dynamic and diverse. In short, you need to stand out. You need to give your users a lasting and unforgettable presence.

The Importance of Social Media Presence

Why is it so important to create an unforgettable presence on social media?

Here's why:

- Consumers do not want regurgitated thoughts. They are not looking for flashy promises or empty content.
- Consumers want real value, originality, and excitement.
- They are looking for content that helps them solve their problems.
- They want to make purchasing decisions on what excites them, what helps them solve a problem.
- According to a study done by NewsCred, 62% of millennials say that their loyalty to a brand is directly connected to the quality of the content that the brands they follow produce.

Keep in mind that millennials have been found to spend $200 billion on annual expenditure. This is an extremely important statistic for marketers to keep in mind.

- It's no more about churning out anything just to have something online.
- You need to dedicate content that relates to your business, supports your brand loyalty, and builds your reputation.
- You want to create an unforgettable social media presence so that you are on the top of your consumer's mind the next time they need their problems solved.
- An unforgotten presence ensures continuous growth and effective communication.
- Your consumers are smart and they are not looking for wishy-washy crud or mediocre posts.

In a high-stakes environment where it is harder than ever before to earn attention online, companies must stand out with EPIC content-superb and well-researched material that adds value solves a customer's problem, and has high quality and relevance.

The Benefits of Being Unforgettable

So, what does quality content bring for the marketer and their brand? What are the benefits of being unforgettable on social media?

The effort we put into our content, our look, and the tone of our brand voice and messaging has everything to do with the bottom line-we want profits, and the only way to make profits is to stand out, and the way to stand out is to create epic content.

Being unforgettable on social media brings in more benefits other than increasing our bottom line. Here are some of them:

- More people will talk about you. It'll earn you more shares online, even get you trending.
- You'll have a better reach of your followers- it'll give you a more relevant, exciting, and actionable data to create better content.
- Being unforgettable online lasts longer and is valuable than ordinary content.

- You reach out to a wider pool of people who have stronger brand loyalty and trust in your company.
- Your brand stands out as a thought leader.
- You get to see how adding that extra time and effort into producing. valuable content produced visible results.
- Boring content doesn't produce results, leaving you wondering where you went wrong.

How Do You Make a Lasting Impression?

You probably have an idea of the regular things marketers do to stand out. It is hard to come up with epic content consistently but there are a few things you can do to stay on top and stay unforgettable, and these are the kinds of things that big brands do anyway on a daily basis.

Here they are:

Define Yourself Online-Develop a Consistent Message, Voice, Look and Feel

Consistently sharing and defining your unique message is extremely relevant and valuable to your target audience. You stand out before your brand look & feel is different, but you also stand out because of the language you use to speak to your audience.

Having a consistent message for your brand will enable users to easily identify you from all that clutter and noise. Everything about your online presence needs to be consistent, from your website to your social media channels, your packaging, layout, and even your online banner ads. Consumers need to recognize you instantly.

You do not want your consumers guessing 'who is this brand?' with every message you post out.

Success in being unforgettable leaves no doubt in the consumer's mind- they know who you are, what you care about, and what your values are. It doesn't matter whether they see your logo on a digital banner or on a billboard.

Keep in mind that these values are not only for big businesses. Whether you are a small business owner, entrepreneur, writer, speaker, or budding business, you need to control the narrative in and around your personal brand.

Build a Captivating Social Media Profile

The wonderful thing about social media profiles is that it helps brands present their stories and messages in a fun, creative, and relatable way. These social media platforms also feed data to search engines. Pinpointing your right target audience, who they are, and what they do so you can craft relevant messages is extremely crucial. This makes it easier for your target audience to find you online.

Use every bit of online retail space as best as possible, whether it's on Pinterest or Google+, Instagram, or even the app store. You want to rock your social media profiles with these important points:

- Make sure you tell people who are as simple and as easy as possible. Don't make them guess. A little creativity goes a long way.
- Add links to your blog, website, or any other place you want your consumers to go to.
- Make your profile relatable, accessible, and authentic- these short sentences should be able to tell a story to the search engines as well as to your audience.

Be Authentic

Nobody said you had to be serious all the time- depending on the context. This really depends on how you want to use your brand and leverage on the context and look and feel you're going for. A summary of yourself, your brand, and what you offer has to be authentic so that your audience relates to you.

When you share something authentic, little facts and tidbits about yourself, your past, your struggle, or even your brand, you end up sparking a conversation. People want to know more about you. The fact that you've struggled in your business or had an embarrassing moment happen makes you human, and that appeals to people who have been through a similar situation. Just when your target audience thought you were not relatable, sharing this little info has enabled them to feel a little closer to you and relate to your voice.

Going Organic

Organic growth is the most sustainable of all. Using relevant keywords in an organic way pushes forth a longer, sustainable outcome. You need to dig deep to find out what terms people search for when they look up the niche you are in, the business pool you operate in as well as the product and service you provide. This information should be sewed into your posts, your content, and your keywords.

Google is eager to search and push the story you want to sell so make sure you help Google find you but adding relevant keywords to create a situation that makes it easy to find you and locate you.

Add in Specific Keywords

Keywords are relevant but they do not create the entirety of the solution. Content sells and adding specific keywords that enable you to stand out in your local area, where customers can reach you easily especially if your product or service is a physical one- is extremely crucial.

- ### *Add Your Call-to-Action*

So, you have your presence set and going on fire, but it will all turn to dust if you do not have a call-to-action to direct your customers to a specific goal you want them to do. Where do you want them to go after viewing your content? What do you want them to click on? Having no place to direct your customers is like getting all dressed up and nowhere to go. Make sure there is a call-to-action on whatever content you are putting out there.

- ***Find Your Uniqueness***

Plenty of successful content creators have found the "one thing" that is their unique identity, that one thing that sells them, that one thing that sets them apart. What's yours? If you haven't figured it out yet, it's ok. As long as you keep working on it, the ideas or the image will become more prevalent. Working with your uniqueness will challenge, excite, and inspire you to continue pushing forth and overcoming whatever challenges there may be.

Conclusion

Thank you for making it through to the end of *Social Media Marketing*, let's hope it was informative and able to provide you with all the tools you need to achieve your goals whatever they may be.

There is no doubt about it, the right social media marketing strategy is going to change your business in ways that you cannot even imagine. There is no better way to build your presence in the digital space than through the immense power of social media. This is one brand awareness and sales tool that you cannot afford to pass up on. Not if you are serious about scaling your business to greater heights, that is.

Social media is a wonderful tool, but it can also prove to be a challenging tool if you don't know where to start. It could also be just as challenging if you are someone who wears multiple hats in your business. Whether your business is big or small, you need social media on your side, that much is clear. Even if you are juggling multiple roles in your business, the key is to identify what aspects of social media you should be focused on to better drive your business. Everything that matters has been covered in this guide. The only thing that is left is for you to get started.

Social media marketing is going to be the very thing that takes your business from mediocre to number one. You want profits, and the only way to make profits is to stand out and the way to stand out is to create epic content, and target the right people with the right strategies. Make a commitment to social media. Make social media marketing a priority for you and your business. Start by planning, create your strategy, create your goals, and identify what success looks like to you. Establish some goals for your social media marketing, and the best thing you can do for your business is to develop goals that align with your social media strategy. Don't forget to be as specific as possible with the details.

More by Santino Spencer

Discover all books from the Marketing Management Series by Santino Spencer at:

bit.ly/santino-spencer

Book 1: Marketing Strategy

Book 2: Business Branding

Book 3: Digital Marketing

Book 4: Social Media Marketing

Book 5: Marketing Analytics

Book 6: Content Marketing

Book 7: Business Development

Book 8: Mobile Marketing

Themed book bundles available at discounted prices:

bit.ly/santino-spencer